JESUS SAVES

A READY TO SING
EASTER

ARRANGED BY RUSSELL MAULDIN
CREATED BY RUSSELL MAULDIN & SUE C. SMITH

AVAILABLE PRODUCTS:

Choral Book 45757-2616-7
CD Preview Pak 45757-2616-1
Listening CD 45757-2616-2
Split-Track Accompaniment CD 45757-2616-3
Audio Stem Files 45757-2616-4
Russell Mauldin Rehearsal DVD 45757-2616-5
Split-Track Accompaniment DVD (Disc 2 contains .Mov files) ... 45757-2616-6
Orchestration/Conductor's Score CD-Rom 45757-2616-8
Soprano Rehearsal Track CD 45757-2617-0
Alto Rehearsal Track CD 45757-2617-5
Tenor Rehearsal Track CD 45757-2617-6
Bass Rehearsal Track CD 45757-2617-7
Bulletins 45757-2617-8
Posters 45757-2617-9

INSTRUMENTATION:

Flute 1, 2 • Oboe • Clarinet 1, 2
F Horn 1, 2 (Alto Sax)
Trumpet 1, 2 • Trumpet 3
Trombone 1, 2 (Tenor Sax/Baritone T.C.)
Trombone 3, 4 • Percussion • Harp
Violin 1, 2 • Viola • Cello • Bass
Synth String Reduction • Rhythm

www.brentwoodbenson.com

BRENTWOOD
MUSIC
PUBLICATIONS

a division of

BRENTWOOD-BENSON
music publications

Contents

Jesus Saves! Opener

Words by
PRISCILLA J. OWENS

Music by
WILLIAM J. KIRKPATRICK
Arranged by Russell Mauldin

This our song of vic-to-ry:

8

Come and See

Words and Music by
MATT REDMAN, CHRIS TOMLIN,
JASON INGRAM and MATT MAHER
Arranged by Russell Mauldin

NARRATOR: Today we'll retell the incredible story of God's plan of redemption. It begins and ends with the matchless love of the Father for the people He created.

(Music starts) It winds its way through the tragedy of the first sin in the Garden of Eden, and spans the lives of men and women who responded in faith to God's work in their world. It goes by way of Bethlehem and Nazareth and Galilee. It reaches a glorious crescendo at Calvary and a garden tomb. There's only one possible title for this epic true account of how good triumphed over evil and love conquered all. This story is called: Jesus Saves.

16

20

77 **18** unis.

to the Light of the world.   You're the Light of the world!_

Fm7   D♭maj7

79

_   In this place,   hearts and lives   wak-ing up

A♭   E♭/G

81 **19** unis.

to the Light of the world.   You're the Light of the world!_

Fm7   D♭maj7

Prepare Ye the Way

Words and Music by
MICHAEL W. SMITH
Arranged by Russell Mauldin

NARRATOR: *(Music starts)* Scripture says that the Lamb who would die to redeem us was "slain from the foundation of the world." Yes, the Father's plan was in place from the beginning. Still, there would be centuries of waiting before His arrival. Prophets foretold His coming with words like, "There will be no end to the increase of His government or of peace, on the throne of David and over His kingdom, to establish it and to uphold it with justice and righteousness from then on and forevermore." *(Isaiah 9:7)*

NARRATOR: As the people God had chosen for Himself strayed further and further from Him, He never gave up on them. The prophets reminded them that their salvation was on the way, saying "Behold, the days are coming," declares the LORD, "when I shall raise up for David a righteous Branch; and He will reign as king and act wisely and do justice and righteousness in the land. In His days Judah will be saved, and Israel will dwell securely; and this is His name by which He will be called, 'The LORD our righteousness.'"
(Jeremiah 23:5-6)

NARRATOR: After 400 years, God's silence was broken by angelic announcements to a priest named Zechariah, a virgin named Mary, and a carpenter named Joseph. The arrival of the Promised One was eminent. And then, there He was: God with us—Jesus, born in Bethlehem. He began His ministry when He was 30 years old. He cared for the poor and the outcast, He healed the sick, and demonstrated His power over the natural world. He taught the people what the promised Kingdom would be like. Yet, all of this wasn't the reason He had come to earth. The time for that was at hand. But first, He would be welcomed into the city of Jerusalem as the King He truly was.

34

We Remember

Words and Music by
RONNIE FREEMAN and SUE C. SMITH
Arranged by Russell Mauldin

*(NOTE: There is an Optional Communion Narration on page 89 for churches
wishing to celebrate communion as a part of their Easter celebration.)*

NARRATOR: It was Passover, the night the nation celebrated how God had miraculously freed them from slavery in Egypt. *(Music starts)* Gathered with His closest friends, Jesus broke the unleavened bread and passed it around, saying, "Take and eat. This is My body." Then He offered the cup, saying, "This is My blood of the covenant, which is poured out for many for the forgiveness of sins." The bread and the wine would be the way we would commemorate the sacrifice He was about to become.

44

Trial and Execution

RUSSELL MAULDIN

NARRATOR: *(Music starts)* Jesus and the Eleven left the room where they had shared the Passover meal and walked to a familiar garden where He often prayed. Judas, the one who betrayed Him, had already gone with the Master's full knowledge of what he was planning. Jesus did nothing to prevent the plot from unfolding. At every step in the hours to come, He would do nothing but surrender to the Father's will.

In the garden, while the disciples slept, He prayed that He wouldn't have to drink the bitter cup of crucifixion. But that would not be the Father's plan, and soon the sound of soldiers and the flames of torches filled Gethsemane. His time had come. He was arrested, bound, and deserted by all His friends.

At His first trial, Jesus stood before Annas, who had been the high priest. At the second, it was the high priest Caiphas who asked Him, "Are you the Christ?" Jesus answered, "I am." At His third trial, He was judged by the Sanhedrin, and at His fourth, Pilate asked, "Are you the King of the Jews?" Jesus answered, "My kingdom is not of this world."

At His fifth trial, it was the brutal King Herod who questioned Him. This man who had beheaded John the Baptist accused Him and berated Him and mocked Him, but Jesus never spoke a word. Herod sent Him back to Pilate, and at His sixth trial of the night, Pilate was pressured into a decision. Though He knew Jesus was guilty of nothing, Pilate gave in to the shouts of the mob who cried "Crucify Him! Crucify Him!" and passed sentence.

Jesus was physically and emotionally exhausted. He endured a brutal Roman scourging and a mock coronation at the hands of the cruel soldiers. Morning had come. He had prayed, "Not My will but Thine be done." Now God's will was unfolding. The Lamb was ready for sacrifice. The altar waited on Golgotha. The cross was prepared.

He Loved Us More
with The Love of God

Words and Music by
GERON DAVIS
Arranged by Russell Mauldin

NARRATOR: There has never been a scene in history like Calvary. *(Music starts)* Artists have attempted to paint it, sculptors have tried to give it form, songwriters have memorialized it over and over, and preachers have delivered its message. Yet the love demonstrated there defies description. The mercy cannot be captured, and the grace is too great to be absorbed. It's more than we can take in, and yet we never stop trying, because the cross and what Jesus did for us there, means everything.

50 *SOLO, with freedom*

Why ___ would a King leave His throne and His crown ___ to come to earth as a stran - ger? And why would He leave the safe - ty of heav - en in ex- change for all earth - ly dan - ger? ____

more than the heav-ens that He called home,

more than the heav-ens that He called home.

more_____ than all of these, He loved you____

Ooo_____

58

60

62

People Need the Lord
with Room at the Cross for You

Words and Music by
GREG NELSON and PHILL McHUGH
Arranged by Russell Mauldin

NARRATOR: *(Music starts)* Are we loved by a God of mercy and forgiveness? Is there a Savior who has made salvation possible? Calvary answers a resounding yes. Yet so many reject the sacrifice of God's only begotten Son. Still He never stops reaching out to them because God knows just how desperately people need Him.

70

ROOM AT THE CROSS FOR YOU (Ira F. Stanphill)

Jesus Saves! Finale

Arranged by Russell Mauldin

NARRATOR: Jesus died and was buried. The crowd at Golgotha left. The disciples hid, His followers mourned, the Jewish leaders sighed with relief, and Jerusalem went back to normal. Then, Sunday dawned! *(Music starts)* An angel rolled back the stone at the tomb, so the world could see that it was empty. The angel said to the women who came to anoint His body, "You're looking for Jesus, who was crucified. He isn't here. He has risen just as He said!"

NARRATOR: All this happened over 2000 thousand years ago, and yet that single event has changed history and the lives of countless souls around the world. We read of Bethlehem, follow His life on earth, hear His words, witness His death on the cross, and we believe in His resurrection. The drumbeat of truth becomes the heartbeat of our lives. It begins as a whisper and rises to a thundering roar: Jesus saves! Jesus saves! Jesus saves!

JESUS SAVES (Travis Cottrell, David Moffitt)

Hear the heart of heav-en beat-ing,___ "Je-sus saves. Je-sus saves." And the hush of mer-cy

82

break - ing, night is quak - ing. God is mak - ing all things

new. Je - sus saves!_____ Je - sus

saves!_____ Oh, to grace, how great a

JESUS SAVES! (Priscilla J. Owens, William J. Kirkpatrick)